Finding the Willpower

A Self-Help Guide to Improving Your Mental Health, Getting Control Over Your Mind and Establishing the Focus You Need to Master Life

Andrew D. Hoskins

Your Gift!

We want to show our appreciation that you support our work,

so we have put together a gift for you.

Just visit the link on the last page of this book to download it

now.

We know you will love this gift.

Thanks!

Table of Content

Introduction

Your mental health is something you should never ignore. But even with that in mind, some people forget about it. This is dangerous as your mind is just as important as your body. You have to keep your mind under control while making the right decisions. It is not always easy but it becomes second nature when you have the willpower needed to change things for the better.

This guide is all about willpower and what you can do to get it. You will learn about how willpower works and the things you should do to get control over your life.

From changing your habits to considering your thoughts, the things that can be done to help you improve your life are vast. This guide is all about helping you to understand what works when you aim to change your life and make it run better.

Read this guide to get a great idea of what you can do for your life. You will be surprised at the many things that can come along in your life when you consider what could work well for your needs. It is impressive to see how well different concepts can work in your life when aiming to resolve many problems that could develop with regards to your attitude.

Chapter 1 – What Is Willpower?

To start, we need to address a simple question – what is willpower, anyway?

Willpower is all about having full control over your thoughts and actions. It focuses on knowing what is right and wrong. Willpower is also about keeping your life in check as you make the right decisions and establish smart routines that you can follow. The things you can do to keep your mind and body in check are heavily dependent on your willpower.

Keeping Thoughts Under Control

Willpower is a necessity for our daily lives. It entails the ability to delay or eliminate thoughts that one does not wish to have. When you have willpower in your life, you are capable of managing control over your actions, words and many other aspects of your life. It is about getting away from the things you do not to be involved with. You will instead focus more on the right things for your life.

Essentially, willpower is all about resisting temptations. When you have the willpower you require, you will help yourself in your quest to attain the long-term goals that you have.

You are not going to give in to certain things that might be satisfying to you right now. Besides, you have better things to think about. You're instead looking at what you know makes your life grow and thrive.

Saying Yes to the Right Things

Part of life involves making the right decisions. You have to make choices that you know are suitable for your life and will help you get far. Those who make the right decisions in their lives are capable of doing more.

This is a key aspect of willpower to look into. Having willpower means being capable of saying yes to what you know is right and appropriate in your life. It is all about avoiding the temptations that come about.

You must have willpower to make it through the world and be a better person all the way around. As you look through this guide, you will read about how you can get the willpower you require for a better overall life.

The Value of Willpower

The key part of willpower is that it gives us the most out of our lives. When we have enough willpower, we show that we are patient and are not willing to rush things along. More importantly, we know what is right and what is wrong.

Let's talk about Walter Mischel's famous marshmallow test for a moment. This is a test that shows just how important willpower truly is.

In Mischel's test, a series of children were presented with marshmallows. But they had to wait a few minutes for someone to return to give them the marshmallows.

Every child that waited properly got two marshmallows. The ones that could not wait and rang a bell asking for marshmallows right away only got one each.

This is a fascinating look into willpower. Those who had more willpower were the ones that could wait for the person to return, thus giving them more marshmallows.

What was interesting is that the children who waited long enough to get two marshmallows were tested years later.

They had better academic testing scores than the ones that only got one marshmallow because they did not have the willpower to wait for that extra one.

Simply put, willpower is critical for your life. Those who have more willpower are more likely to have control over their thoughts. They know how to make good decisions and are not ready to make rash moves or make other difficult choices.

More importantly, you will feel happier when you have the willpower you require. As you have willpower, you will be more likely to feel satisfaction. It all comes as you have a better chance at getting things you want.

The patience and strength you hold will be worthwhile as you are capable of getting everything you wish for. The control and effort you put into your life is a necessity to look into.

Chapter 2 – Be Aware of Yourself

How many choices do you think you make in a typical day? The odds are you make hundreds of choices from when you wake up to when you get to sleep.

The amazing thing is that we are not fully aware of some of the decisions that we make. We don't think about our choices when getting foods ready, choosing what roads we go down when driving and so forth.

The worst part is that it is not all that easy for you to be aware of some of the decisions you make. You might be on auto-pilot because you are not thinking all that much about what you are doing.

Self-awareness is critical for your life. This refers to recognizing what you are doing as you are doing it.

As you become aware, you will identify things that need to change. This in turn improves upon how well you can change your attitude.

Consider Your Life Story

Be ready to look back at your life. Think about the earliest memories you have. Look at what made the most important in your life and how certain things changed it for the better. Frame those thoughts into ideas for what you want to get out of your life. Allow those thoughts to create frameworks for the positive things you want to look into.

Be willing to look back at your life and see what has made it so spectacular. You will surely be surprised over the good things that come out of it.

Sure, it might be difficult for you to think about some of the stuff that came about in your life. But you just need to look at what you are getting within your life so it becomes easier for you to develop a plan for improving upon your life.

Review Your Surroundings

Think about your surroundings when you go places or do things in your daily life. What surrounds you on a daily basis? What things are impacted the most by what you get into? Who is influenced by your decisions?

Think about everything that surrounds you and see what you can do to change your life for the better. Consider how other people will be positively or negatively impacted by what you are doing.

Willpower involves having a sense of sympathy for those who are influenced by what you are doing with your life. Be ready to address the problems that come about with certain actions and find ways to resolve those issues.

Address the Thoughts That Come In

Watch for the new thoughts you come across as you go about your day. Be willing to acknowledge any new things you experience.

As new thoughts come about, ask yourself if what you are feeling or thinking is logical or sensible. Look at how unusual some of those thoughts might be. Think about whether or not these are logical or easy to follow.

More importantly, look at how realistic those thoughts are. Are the things you are thinking about true? Are you assuming things that might not necessarily be right?

Looking at the thoughts you experience in your day always helps. You will go far in your life if you just think about what comes into your mind all the time.

Do not be afraid of looking into every single thought that comes into your mind. Even the smallest thoughts might make a real difference. Some of those thoughts might give you clear ideas on things that might have changed your life.

Pause Between Things You Do

Think about what you are doing with your life after you do certain things in your daily routine. Review what you have just done and see what you think could have been changed around for the better.

Take time to reflect on the things that you do. When you take a close inventory of your life, you will find it is not all that hard to get more out of it. You will get a clear idea of what you are doing based on what is right for your life and what is hurting yourself.

This extra bit of time gives you the opportunity to look into what might have changed in your life and how well certain actions could develop. It becomes very easy for you to make better decisions as you get a clear idea of what could be to your liking or benefit in life.

The consequences of what you are doing should be easier to notice when you just take a moment to pause between the things that you are doing. You may start to notice some of the immediate effects that come with what you are getting yourself into.

It should be easy for you to get the willpower you need as you look at what you are doing with your life. You will feel confident in your life when you know how to handle it while understanding what impacts your decisions and actions make.

Chapter 3 – Develop Strong Habits

Willpower is all about making good choices. As you develop your willpower, you will be less likely to make rash decisions. One way how you could develop your willpower is by looking at the habits you get yourself into. Think about how you are creating strong and appealing habits that influence your life for the better.

You must have great habits if you wish to make the right choices in your life. Willpower is often about establishing a stronger attitude where you will not be likely to make bad moves.

Incorporate Things Into Your Regular Routine

One way to start putting in good habits is to add positive behaviors and activities into your daily routine. Whether it entails working out or eating healthy, you should look at the good things that could make your life better and then add them into your routine.

To start, set up a plan where you drink water while working. You might consider adding periods of time in the day when you take a break from tasks for a bit of water. This could help you with staying active while keeping you from drinking anything unhealthy like alcohol or soft drinks. It also keeps you focused on what you want to do.

Add such actions into your routine so you don't forget about them. After a while, you will become more likely to partake in certain actions without having to be reminded.

This part of improving your willpower involves thinking more about the positive things that come out of certain habits. The simplicity to following certain tasks helps to improve upon what you are getting out of your life.

As you incorporate such positive things into your routine, it becomes easier for you to get used to certain tasks. This keeps the stresses in your daily life under control. You might even have a little more control over what you want to get out of it.

Do think about the things that you add into your life and that you are not overly complicated though. Do not stick with stuff that might be tough to follow. While you could engage in plenty of positive changes, it is best to look at how you could change your life for the better with things that you know are actually possible.

Do not try and be something you are not. Stick with new things that you know are reasonable and do not put you at risk of any serious problems.

Avoid Delaying Things

Have you ever had one of those days where you struggle to try and get up in the morning? Maybe you are thinking about all the stuff that you have to do and that you really just want to rest for a bit.

Those who do not have the willpower to get things done and live stronger lives are more likely to delay things in their lives. This only makes it harder for them to live better.

Procrastination is a plague that makes life hard. You might consider putting certain things off until later. You could do this with the belief that you can take care of particular tasks later on.

But in reality, the amount of time you have to complete those tasks is significantly reduced. It becomes harder for you to do things because you have no time to waste. As a result, you might rush through certain tasks or put in a half-effort job just to say you completed something.

Delaying your work only adds to your stress. Instead of delaying it, put your willpower into finishing off certain jobs. Figure out times for when you will complete certain jobs. Schedule those times to start as soon as possible. Allow for extra time for you to finish things. You might think that your window of time for completing things seems large at the start but it would be easier for you to finish your tasks if you just put in an extra amount of effort into the process.

Be ready to keep working and doing more with your life. You might find that your life is better when you just think about what you know works well.

Chapter 4 – Relax For a Moment

One way for you to develop willpower is to relax. This does not mean you should just establish a regular sleep schedule where you can get the rest you require. Naturally, you will need to get that rest but relaxation entails more than just resting.

Certain activities will give you more control over your life. These help you clear your mind so you have more control over all the good things you want to do with it.

Meditation

Meditation has long been an activity among those who simply want to be one with who they are. The key part of meditation is that it helps you focus on what you are thinking.

As you meditate, you become more aware of your breathing and your inner monologues. You start to feel more in control over your life and what you want to think. This gives you extra help for keeping your life in check.

Meditation gives you an extra bit of time to think about what you want out of life and how you are going to live it. You will be impressed at how well your life can change and how strong it can be if you just clear your mind. Training yourself through meditation is important to do.

Check with local schools or recreational centers to learn about how you can meditate. Various places offer meditation classes to help you understand the ins and outs that come with working out.

Yoga

Yoga is a little more complicated that meditation. Yoga entails the use of physical poses that go alongside breathing exercises. Such an activity as this is popular for having many physical benefits. In particular, yoga helps you to strengthen your muscles and to become more flexible. But the mental benefits that come with yoga are worthwhile.

Specifically, you will boost your willpower when you engage in yoga. As you get into the proper positions, you place a stronger emphasis on the present. You begin to develop a sense of awareness of things around you. Your thoughts become a little easier to control and process. Part of this focuses heavily on changing your attitudes and actions.

With yoga, you start thinking more about what makes a real difference in your life. You begin to feel confident in your ability to manage your thoughts. This in turn gives you an extra amount of control over what you want to get out of life. Yoga is very complex and detailed. Check with a local yoga studio to learn more about how yoga works and what you can do to improve your life through this fine activity.

Tai Chi

Tai chi is another relaxing activity similar to what you might get out of yoga. Tai chi is an activity where you move your body through a series of slow movements.

The key part of tai chi is to get into a series of gentle and carefully orchestrated positions. You must enter into those positions while focusing on your breathing.

This is a routine that helps build upon your physical concentration. It also gives you more control over your mind as you think about your surroundings and your mental processes. As everything becomes a little more controlled, you start to think about what is around you and what you might have come across in the day.

Tai chi is another great activity that is taught by various schools and clinics around the country. Check your local area to see what is available.

Remember that relaxation should entail more than just getting the recommended amount of sleep that you need each night. This also involves getting into comfortable activities that help you reset your mind and expand upon your focus. As you do this, it becomes easier for you to develop a great life with the willpower you need for success.

Chapter 5 – Plan Your Life Properly

Another part of getting willpower involves knowing how you are going to life your life. You might be surprised at how well it could change if you think about your willpower.

Think about your life and what you want to do with it. Look at how you are planning certain activities so you understand the needs that you hold for your general success in life.

Prepare a Schedule

Start by looking at what you do on a regular basis. Plan a good schedule for your life so it becomes easier for you to sustain your mental processes.

Do not just pile everything together at once though. Get to work with a sensible schedule where you can divide projects or efforts into a few series of points. Keeping what you want to do under control is always worthwhile as you fully understand what you want to do with yourself.

Figure out your schedule by looking at the most important things you want to do in your day. Add details on how much of an effort you want to place into your work. Choose carefully so you will have more control over what you want to get out of your efforts in general.

Be flexible with your schedule but make sure you have smart deadlines. These include deadlines that you can actually follow. This leads to the next point worth noting.

Establish Good Deadlines

Figure out your plans for your schedule by setting deadlines that you know are not all that complicated. Keep tabs on what you have to do. Think about how much time you have to complete everything you want to finish.

Be realistic when figuring out your deadlines. You do not want to force yourself into doing the work of three or four people at a time. But even when getting deadlines ready, make sure you avoid shifting those plans.

Prepare firm deadlines that you know are easy to meet and cannot be shifted. As you do this, you will feel motivated to do certain things as soon as possible. This improves upon your chances for getting particular tasks completed well.

This also helps you to train your willpower as you will think more about finishing certain routines or efforts a little sooner. This bit of motivation could make a real impact as you try to change your life for the better.

As you read a little earlier, procrastination only makes things harder for you to complete. Getting things done as soon as possible is the best thing you can do. It is all about keeping your life under control without being at risk of hurting your emotional attitude.

Set Up Plans For What You Do

As you go along with your life, think about the alternatives that you could utilize when making certain decisions. For instance, you might consider eating something healthier for lunch that might take a bit of extra time to prepare but will still be better than junk food that might be easier to eat but still harmful to your body.

As you have a plan for your actions, you will feel less stress. You will have a better idea of what you will get out of your life. More importantly, you will be in more control over your life. Instead of being uncertain over the things you want to do, you will have a solid plan set up where you have a clear idea of what is right for your life.

Thanks to these plans, it becomes easier for you to establish a stronger life. You will not be at much of a risk of harm when you think about what you are getting from your life.

Stay Accountable

As you plan your life, keep yourself accountable for everything that happens. Do not blame other people if things do not work out as well as they should. It is you that is responsible for everything good and bad that comes about.

A good idea is to keep a journal that reviews everything you do in a typical day. Write about the things that you do in that day and figure out what you have done that works well. Talk about your stresses and everything you feel as you go through your routine.

While writing your journal, you will notice that there are many aspects of your life that might be very difficult to manage. You might see that some of your fears or worries are not going away as easily as they should.

As you work on your journal, you will get a clear idea of what is going right in your life versus what needs to change for the better. This sense of accountability lets you figure out some of the things that might be better for your life without being tough to follow.

Don't Forecast Things

Forecasting is often done by people who want to think about stuff that might come along later on in time. People who forecast things often struggle in their lives because they are too busy thinking about stuff that might not happen.

You have to avoid forecasting things that might come about. Do not think about stuff that you feel could happen because there is never a guarantee that the stuff you are worried about will come true.

Planning your life is not too hard to handle if you just think about what you have to do. Get a great schedule ready so you will have more control over your life and a better sense of motivation. This is all about training you to get the most out of life without being too hard to follow.

Chapter 6 – Keeping Negative Thoughts Under Control

One issue that often keeps people from having the willpower they need entails negative thoughts. It is very easy for such bad thoughts to go around and bother people.

Negative ideas always discourage people from doing certain things. They might think less about themselves and more about what can go wrong.

This makes it harder for people to have the willpower needed to get through the day. Sometimes a person who has negative thoughts will make rash decisions without thinking. Such choices might make matters worse.

It is not impossible for you to keep such negative thoughts from being a threat. A few things should be done to help you keep these thoughts in check.

Journal Your Bad Thoughts

You already read a bit ago about how a journal can help you organize your thoughts and actions. Such a journal can also help you see where your bad thoughts are coming from.

Write down your bad feelings and the issues you come across in your life. Discuss what caused you to feel these things and what might be keeping you from keeping your mind straight. As you write things down, start looking into any trends that might influence what you are thinking. Look at points like why you are thinking about something or what is triggering such actions. You might have to change your behaviors around to keep you from feeling these thoughts.

Look at how long such thoughts stick around for. Over time, you should start to see those thoughts being less common. You might need to ask someone for extra help if you struggle with certain problems. This includes asking for help with understanding how to fix certain problems.

Are Those Negative Feelings True?

Look for a moment at what is causing you to feel certain things. Are the negative feelings you are coming across really all that true?

People often develop negative feelings because they are not aware of what is real and what is not. They focus far too much on some of the bad things that develop in their minds because they do not spend enough time sorting out their thoughts. They just assume that all the bad things that come along in their lives are just actions that will come about.

Ask yourself if the bad thoughts you have are true and if they are logical.

You might find that some of those attitudes are not doing much of anything for your life.

After a while, you might notice that those negative feelings will go away rather quickly. You will have more sense in your life as you begin to eliminate some of the bad attitudes or thoughts that you once had.

Do Not Take Things Personally

Sometimes the negative things that come about in your life might hit close to home. They might relate to your mental or physical inabilities or things that might be extremely difficult for you to do.

You should never take any negative attitudes or emotions you develop personally. Taking such things personally only hurts as it makes you feel overly hard on yourself.

Look at any negative thought that comes along and see if it is something that relates to what you are doing. You must avoid associating such things with whatever you might already be doing with your life. You will notice after a while that some of those things you think are just stuff that comes about at random.

Being able to handle the negative thoughts you come across is critical to your ability to have a better life. Your willpower will improve when you keep those bad feelings in check.

Chapter 7 – Rewarding Yourself

As you work towards building willpower, you should give yourself a few rewards for a job well done. Giving yourself special rewards for good actions is always smart to do.

As you reward yourself, it becomes easier for you to stay motivated. You will keep aiming to improve upon your life and make it stand out a little more.

Establish a Reward System

Start by looking at a reward system you can live with. Such a system will entail a review of great things you might want to get in your life.

For instance, you might be trying to get more work done around the house. You might have a desire to clean out and clear off many spaces in your home or even start a larger renovation project.

Think about the rewards you could provide yourself with after you finish those tasks around your home. Establish a reward schedule that focuses on things like what you could buy as a reward for special activities outside the home you could partake in. You could set up schedule rewards after you complete particular activities.

Smaller rewards can be utilized after you complete minor tasks. The largest and most significant ones may come along after you have finished more complicated or difficult tasks.

A reward system establishes a good layout where you are

focusing more on the great things you want to add into your life. You will know that by making the right decisions and keeping your eyes on the prize, you will get what you want. That all relates back to the marshmallow study you read about earlier. Every good thing in life requires a bit of extra effort to make it happen. Creating a good reward system makes it easier for you to get a better life up and running.

Give People More

Another way to reward yourself is to give more of what you have to offer to other people. Whether it entails helping people with certain tasks or giving them resources that they need for any intention, you might be impressed at how happy your friends will be when you give them the help they demand. For instance, a friend might need a bit of help with a home improvement project. You could head out to that friend's house to offer some assistance with that project. This gives you the opportunity to help someone with certain tasks that might be complicated or detailed.

In return, your friend will be likely to reward you with something. It might be some tangible good or even future considerations for when you need help with something important in the future.

More importantly, you could reward yourself by having a better friendship with someone. You will give yourself a more positive as you are showing someone that you care and that you are worth something.

This in turn eliminates many negative thoughts you might have. It becomes harder for those thoughts to persist as well, thus giving you the reward of having more control over your mind and where you want to go with it.

Sustain Your Willpower

A great reward schedule assists you in keeping your willpower under control. It should be easier for your life to stay intact with a better attitude all the way through but only if you think about your willpower and how you will develop it over time. Preparing a great reward system always gives you a bit of extra help for your life. It is easier for you to stick with a plan for improving your willpower when you think of the incentives that come about when you set up a great attitude and sense of control in your life.

Chapter 8 – Seeking Support

This guide has provided you with plenty of pointers for getting the most out of your willpower. But it might be better for you to get a bit of outside help in the process.

Getting support from other people always helps. The extra help you get from other people will give you the motivation and encouragement you require for your general success. This is important if you are trying to complete certain difficult tasks or you need just an extra bit of help for getting a project running well.

Support Groups Help

Look for support groups that can assist you with attaining the willpower you need for completing certain goals in your life. Such groups include people who have goals just like you and are often let by people who have attained success and have been in your shoes before.

Such support groups are ideal if you are trying to do something really significant like quitting smoking. The emotional support you get out of other people will make a huge difference.

Do not be afraid to share your concerns with others in a

support group. Being open helps as you make yourself more receptive to great ideas.

Discuss Your Plans With Friends and Family Members

You do not want to go after your efforts without letting others know what you want to do. Talk with friends and family members about what you are trying to do with your life. Let them know about your goals and what you want to do to get your willpower under control.

Share details on your goals and ask them to help you out if possible. For instance, if you are trying to get the willpower needed to avoid overeating then ask family members to not prepare loads of dangerous foods while you visit them. Let them assist you with getting your body in check without putting you at risk of further harm.

Ask For Feedback

Talk with other people about what you are doing with your life. Ask them what they think about your efforts and habits for living. You might be surprised by the positive feedback you get on occasion.

But even criticism can help. Those who are willing to address issues you have in your life are always there to help you out. They want to give you advice for having a better life that you can follow. They will understand that you need a bit of a push to go somewhere and get the most out of your work.

Do not be afraid to ask other people for help. Sometimes a bit of encouragement or support from people who are close to you will make the most impact in your efforts.

Conclusion

Getting the willpower you need to bolster your mind is a necessity for your life. You must prepare your mind and body carefully so you can change it for the better.

Look at what you are trying to do when getting the willpower you require. Think about the actions you partake in and the feelings you experience.

Be ready to plan your life with certain activities or concepts in mind. Allow yourself to have more control over your life while figuring out the ways how you can make it better.

As you develop a stronger sense of willpower, you will find that your life is better for it. You will start to make better decisions without rushing into things all that often. You will also become more responsible and positive about yourself.

Be sure you use the pointers in this guide often. You will certainly notice how great your life can be when you just think about the good stuff that could come along after a while.

Your Gift!

We want to show our appreciation that you support our work, so we have put together a gift for you.

bit.ly/2xXbHO5

Just visit the link above to download it now.

We know you will love this gift.
Thanks!